COSMO'S AQUA KAMA SUTRA

COSMO'S AQUA KAMA SUTRA

25 sex positions for the tub, shower, pool, and more

The Editors of COSMOPOLITAN

Illustrations by BO LUNDBERG

Hearst Books
A Division of Sterling Publishing Co., Inc.
New York

Contents

■ Lust Lessons

COSMO'S LUST LOCALE KEY

Use these symbols to pick the perfect hot spot for each pose.

BATHTUB

HOT TUB

SHOWER

SPRINKLER

POOL

LAKE

OCEAN

Preface

If there's one thing *Cosmo* knows, it's that there's nothing better than great sex. But how do you keep your carnal encounters hot all the time? One word: *experimentation*.

That's why we suggest occasionally bringing in a third body…of water that is. Whether it's a hot tub, a swimming pool, the shower, the ocean, or hell, in your backyard while standing over a sprinkler, having sex in any of these wet-and-wild locales can add an extra erotic splash to your lust life.

Before you start flipping through these pages, we need to warn you that getting busy in the water can be trickier than in the bedroom. That's why *Cosmo* crafted a Water-Sex Wisdom primer—a must-read that will help you deal with potential pitfalls while maximizing the pleasure you and your man experience (see Lust Lesson #1 on page 8).

As you both prepare to sail through these 25 mind-blowing poses—from the extra-naughty Deep-Water Dare to the adventurous Surf's Up—you'll want to be sure to consult *Cosmo's* Lust Locale Key (see the previous page) to find out the best place to try each position. In many cases, we recommend more than one!

Plus, there are five additional Lust Lessons—on topics ranging from the hottest waterproof sex toys for spicing up your sack sessions to aqua foreplay games that will have you and your guy aching for each other.

And here's the real bonus: *Cosmo's Aqua Kama Sutra* is 100 percent waterproof, so you can bring this randy reference along wherever the tide takes you!

What are you waiting for? Dive in....

—The Editors of *Cosmopolitan*

Water-Sex Wisdom

Here's everything you need to know about playing it safe while trying the aqua poses in this book.

Condom Conundrum

Protecting yourself against pregnancy and STDs underwater is more challenging than on dry land. Some of the potential problems:

● Putting on a condom is difficult to do in water. And once he manages to get it on, water can seep in through the base, causing it to slip off.

● Products you may want to use during your erotic aqua adventure (such as bubble bath, shampoo, or sunscreen) can break down latex condoms, which are the most popular kind.

● There's no data about how water or the chemicals used in pools and hot tubs affect condoms.

To play it safe, you should use a condom anyway. Or, better yet, save aqua sex for someone with whom you have a monogamous relationship—who you know is STD free—and use another form of birth control besides condoms.

Lube Lowdown

Ironically, having sex in water dries out your natural lubrication, which can cause uncomfortable friction during penetration. The solution: Use plenty of silicone-based lube, which is completely waterproof, making it ideal for underwater sex. Reapply as often as necessary.

THE LUSTY LIMBER-UP

Using a towel for resistance, these moves will get you ready for any position.

THE MOVE	WHAT IT WORKS	HOW IT'S DONE
Treasure Chest	Chest, shoulders, upper back, biceps	Stand with feet hip-width apart, and hold the end of a twisted towel in each hand. Raise your arms, then pull the towel taut slightly behind your head. Hold for 45 seconds, relax, and repeat two more times.
Thigh High	Calves, hamstrings, quads	Lie on your back with knees bent. Raise your right leg, placing the towel over the ball of your foot. Gently pull the towel down. Hold for 45 seconds, release tension, then switch legs.
Butt Booster	Front of hips, butt, thighs	Place your feet hip-width apart. Keeping your arms fully extended in front of you and holding the towel with both hands, squat and slowly raise yourself back up. Do 12 squats, rest, and repeat.

JACK MISKELL

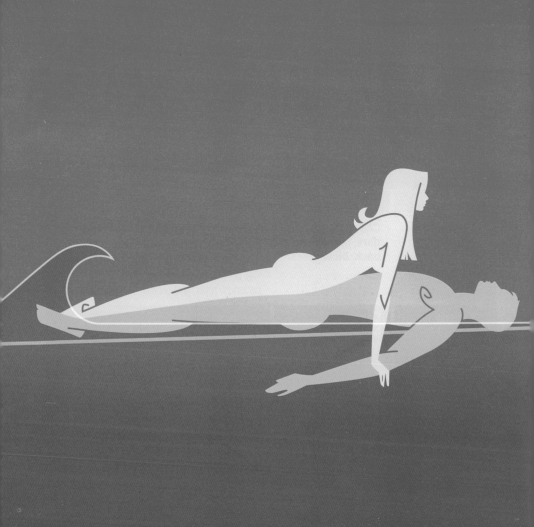

Torrid Tidal Wave

■ Erotic Instructions

Use this pose to turn a make-out session on a secluded beach into an unforgettable sex session. Have your man lie on his back at the water's edge, keeping his legs straight and together. Lie on top of him with your pelvises aligned, then take his penis inside you. Lift your torso, resting your weight on your hands, and move up and down.

■ Why You'll Love It

With every push, your clitoris rubs against his pelvic bone, creating toe-clenching friction. Plus, each cascading wave of the ocean sends sensation-boosting currents over your bodies.

AQUA EXTRA

Sporadically clench your butt cheeks really tight for a few seconds so you'll be able to feel his penis inside you even more intensely.

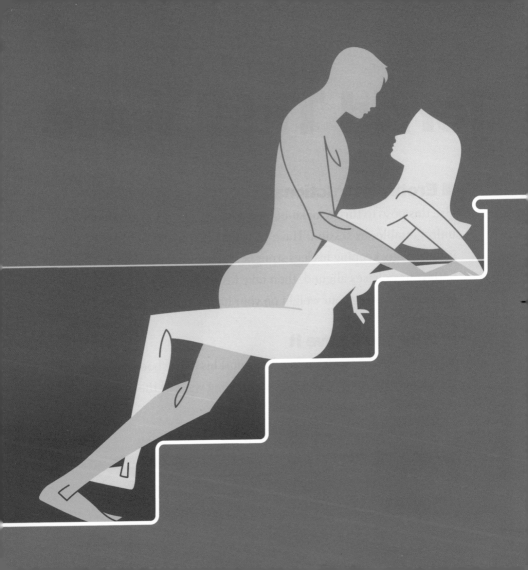

Stairway to Heaven

■ Erotic Instructions

Sit on the second-to-last stair in the shallow end of the pool with your legs spread. Lean back on your forearms for support. Have your man stand between your legs with his arms on either side of you as he enters you. He can lean on his hands for leverage as he thrusts wildly.

■ Why You'll Love It

Your man's vigorous in-and-out movements will create carnal currents that will hit your nether regions, boosting stimulation.

AQUA EXTRA

To get more up close and personal, lean forward, wrap your hands around his neck, and pull him in for some sensual smooching.

Deep-Water Dare

■ Erotic Instructions

When you and your guy are swimming, make your way to chest-high water and stand face-to-face. Hold on to his shoulders as you jump up and wrap your legs tightly around his thighs. Have him cradle your butt with both hands to keep you propped up as he enters you. The water will make you weightless so you can easily glide back and forth.

■ Why You'll Love It

This pose is discreet enough to try out in a lake or the ocean without getting caught. And there's nothing like the thrill of doing it outside. Just knowing that you're being a little bit bad amps up the excitement.

AQUA EXTRA

Make sure you don't wind up bare-assed by letting your bikini bottom wash out to sea: Push it to the side instead of taking it all the way off.

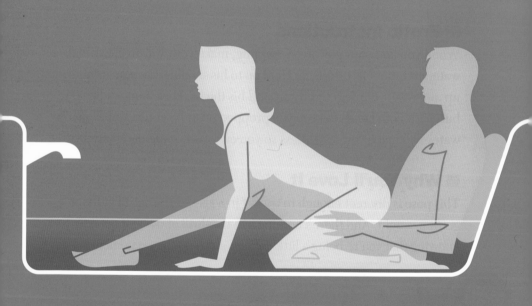

Bathtub Boogie

■ Erotic Instructions

Your partner reclines in the tub with the water level waist high. If he's too tall to straighten his legs, he can bend them. Place an inflatable bath pillow behind his back if you have one. Then straddle his lap, facing his feet, and slowly lower yourself onto his penis. Lean forward so you're resting on your palms. He holds on to your butt or thighs as you ride him.

■ Why You'll Love It

You're steering the ship, so you control the speed and depth of penetration to ensure maximum pleasure for you. He gets to indulge his voyeuristic tendencies with a randy rear view, which will really float his boat.

AQUA EXTRA

This is a primo opportunity for some good, clean fun. Have him soap up his hands and massage your tush and lower back into a lusty lather.

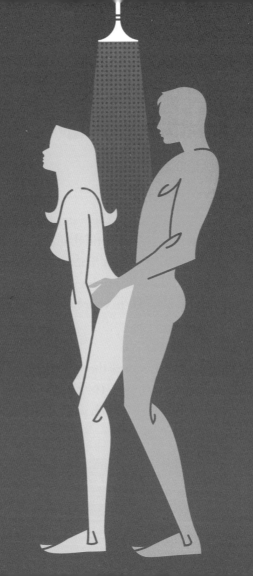

Slippery When Wet

■ Erotic Instructions

Stand facing the side of the tub directly under the showerhead (with water running). Lean slightly forward, keeping your back straight and your hands on your thighs. Your man stands behind you and holds your waist as he enters you. He can intensify the action by pulling you back and forth.

■ Why You'll Love It

This passion pose under the showerhead allows the water to spray the point of entry, creating even more pulsating sensations as he thrusts.

AQUA EXTRA

Add a little manual action and stimulate your clitoris, or reach between your legs and give him a sexy surprise by fondling his highly sensitive testicles.

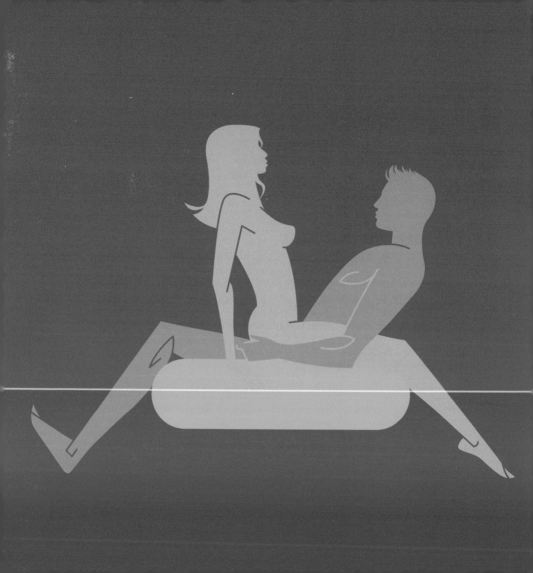

Tawdry Tube

■ Erotic Instructions

Have your guy sit in an inner tube with his legs dangling over the edge. Then straddle his lap while facing him, and slowly lower yourself onto his penis with your hands on his shoulders or the tube for support. Once he's inside you, begin to rock back and forth. He can intensify the action by grasping your hips to help propel you.

■ Why You'll Love It

This face-to-face position is seriously intimate. Since the tube is hollow in the middle, the splashing water created by your thrusting hits both of your down-there domains, adding to the titillation.

AQUA EXTRA To put yourself in a better G-spotting pose, change the angle of penetration by placing your legs over his shoulders and leaning back.

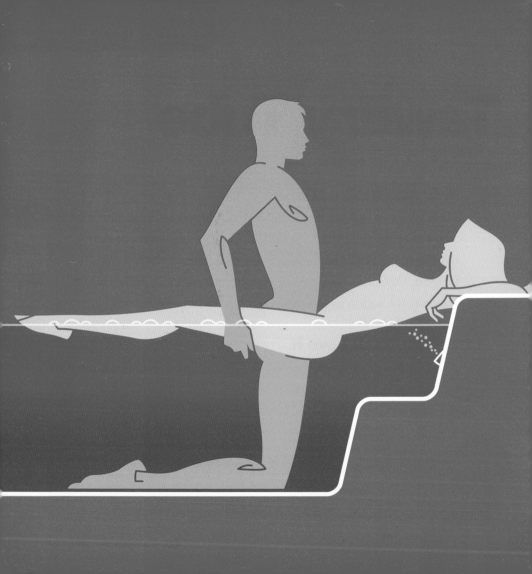

Bubbly Back Float

■ Erotic Instructions

Recline in a hot tub with your arms stretched out to your sides, holding on to the edge of the tub for support if you need to. Your partner kneels between your legs, facing you, and lifts you by the backs of your thighs so you're floating off the seat and he can enter you.

■ Why You'll Love It

Floating weightlessly gives you pelvic flexibility. You can experiment with aqua acrobatics that you couldn't manage on solid ground.

AQUA EXTRA

Situate yourself in front of a jet so the bubbles circulate below you, creating a tickly carnal current that will amp up the pleasure.

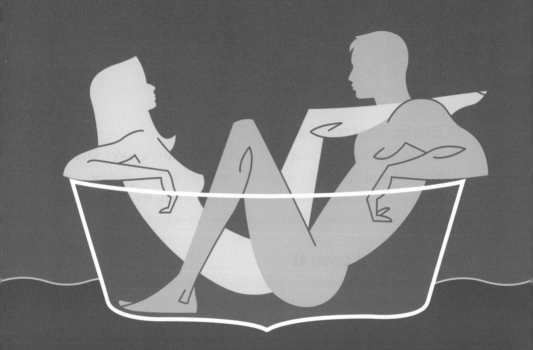

Rock His Boat

■ Erotic Instructions

Have your guy sit against the side of a small boat. He should lean back and keep his knees bent and legs apart while resting his arms on the edge of the boat. Straddle his lap and take him inside you. Carefully lean away from him and place your legs over his shoulders. Then slowly rock back and forth until you both fall into a randy rhythm.

■ Why You'll Love It

With the boat rocking beneath you and the water splashing, every move you two make will be magnified. For some, the potential for tipping over will up the thrill factor.

AQUA EXTRA

If leaning back becomes uncomfortable, you can switch positions by lowering your legs and embracing each other in a bear hug.

Wet Warm-Up

If aqua sex seems too challenging, use the water for fun foreplay games, then hit the bedroom.

Tub Tease

Slide in to a warm bath with your naked man behind you. Take turns slowly lathering each other up. Have him trace sexy circles around your breasts, belly, and inner thighs. Then switch, and run your hand from his chest down to his abs and gently up and down his penis. Concentrate on stroking the underside of the shaft and along the frenulum (the ultra-sensitive ridge right below the head).

Spray Play

Grab a hose (at the kitchen sink or in the backyard) and surprise your man with a sudden spritz. Then turn the spray on yourself so your top clings to you, giving him a view of your erect nipples. Take things to a lustier level by rubbing your breasts and stomach before inviting him to join you.

Fun in the Sun

Sex up a day at the beach with an SPF-slathering massage. Have your guy lie on his stomach, and starting at his shoulders, work your way down his back using long, sensual strokes. The sensation of the cool lotion on his hot skin will send shivers down his spine. If no one's watching, let your fingers graze the inside of his shorts. Then, lead him to the water. Once you're submerged, continue your in-his-trunks exploration, alternating between rubbing his shaft and fondling his testicles.

AQUA ACCOUTREMENTS

These "toys" will make your sessions buzz-worthy.

Bathtime Sponge	In the tub or shower, have your man run this sexy yellow sponge (with a vibrator inside of it) all over your body. For maximum orgasmic impact, let him tease you silly and hold off on hitting your main moan zone until the last minute.
Lucky Duck	This little critter might look like a cute plaything, but it is definitely not meant for kids. The round head, pointed tail, and nubby beak offer a variety of contact textures to hit all of your hot spots (and your man's too).
Body Glow	No ordinary loofah, this skin buffer has an internal waterproof vibrating bullet. It's the perfect passion prop for exfoliating—and titillating—you from head to toe.
Water Bunny	This ever-popular randy rabbit is waterproof and doubles your pleasure by turning on two sensual spots on your body at once. One part massages your clitoris; the other provides you with inner satisfaction. The result is sheer bliss.

PRODUCTS CAN BE FOUND AT ADULT BOUTIQUES AND ONLINE AT SITES LIKE MYPLEASURE.COM AND BABELAND.COM.

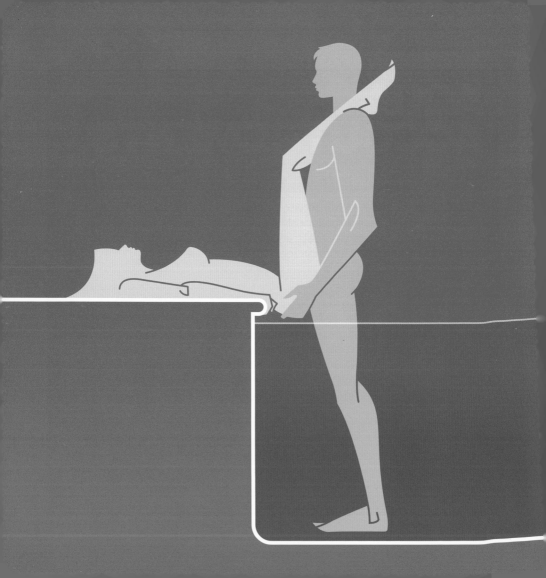

On the Edge

■ Erotic Instructions

Lie on your back by the edge of a pool or dock so your butt's just hanging over the edge above the water. Have your man stand in the water, facing you, then lift your legs and rest them on his shoulders as he enters you. You can hold on to the edge of the pool or dock for support.

■ Why You'll Love It

With On the Edge, your man has a full frontal view. So up the optic ante (and channel your inner sex goddess) by caressing your breasts and tummy, which will give him even more eye candy. A bonus: You'll feel spasms of pleasure as the cool water splashes your privates.

AQUA EXTRA

Place your hands under the small of your back to lift your pelvis, which puts you in the perfect pose for even deeper thrusting and G-spot stimulation.

Breaking the Waves

■ Erotic Instructions

Your partner sits cross-legged at the shoreline or in shallow water. Straddle his lap with your knees planted on either side of him as you lower yourself onto his member. Rest your hands on his shoulders, and have him place his hands on your butt so he can help you move up and down.

■ Why You'll Love It

Being on your knees keeps you balanced, so it's a cinch for you to change things up with back-and-forth and circular gyrations.

AQUA EXTRA

Sync up your bumping-and-grinding with the ebb and flow of the tide so the incoming waves can help propel you into a very randy rhythm.

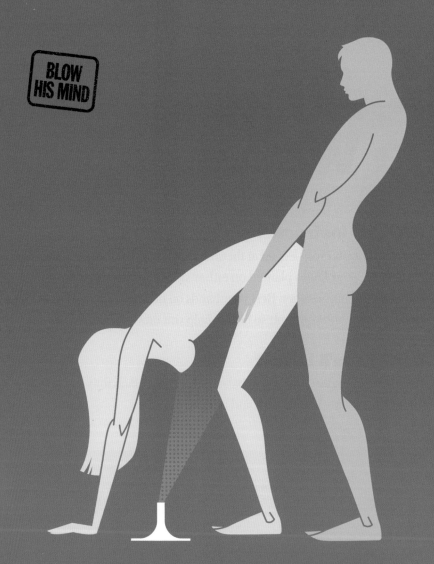

Sexy Sprinkler

■ Erotic Instructions

Save this position for a day (or night) when you two have the backyard to yourselves. Stand beside a soft-spraying sprinkler and bend over so the water hits your genitals. If you can't reach your hands to the ground, place them on your thighs or calves for support. Your partner should stand behind you and put his hands around your waist as he enters you.

■ Why You'll Love It

The sprinkler provides the same kind of clitoral stimulation as a handheld nozzle (see The Rub-a-Dub on page 44). And the aroma of wet grass boosts your sense of smell, making this a supersensory experience.

AQUA EXTRA

Instead of keeping the sprinkler on the stationary setting, switch it to rotate so you get a bliss-inducing blast all over your body.

Get a Leg Up

■ Erotic Instructions

Fill the tub with only a few inches of water, then turn on the shower and let it run lightly. Lie on your side, propped up on your forearm. (Bend your knee if you need to.) Lift your top leg, then have your man straddle your other leg. Once he's entered you, rest your lifted leg on his shoulder as he holds on to your elevated thigh for leverage.

■ Why You'll Love It

With your guy crouching between your legs, his pelvic bone rubs against your clitoris, treating you to a double dose of bliss. And, the cascading water hits both your bodies, showering you with massaging droplets.

AQUA EXTRA

Work him into a frenzy by stroking and lightly scratching his inner thigh. When he's near climax, gently tug his boys to send him over the edge.

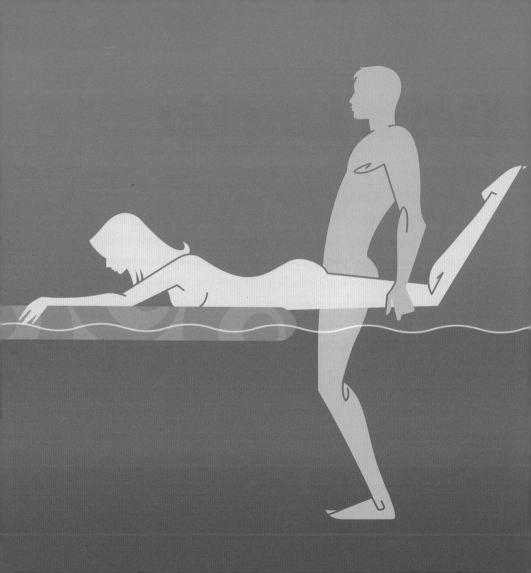

Randy Raft

■ Erotic Instructions

Climb onto a well-inflated raft in shallow water, and lie on your stomach with your butt and legs dangling over the edge. Your man should grab on to your thighs, as if he were pushing a wheelbarrow, then enter you. He can then pull you incredibly close for the deepest possible penetration.

■ Why You'll Love It

The Randy Raft delivers a double whammy. First, your guy can move your legs up and down to vary the angle of penetration, creating alternating sensations for you. Plus, since you can't see him, you aren't able to anticipate his next move, which is surprisingly thrilling.

AQUA EXTRA As your man gets close to climaxing, have him lean forward so his chest is pressed against your back for an intimate skin-to-skin finale.

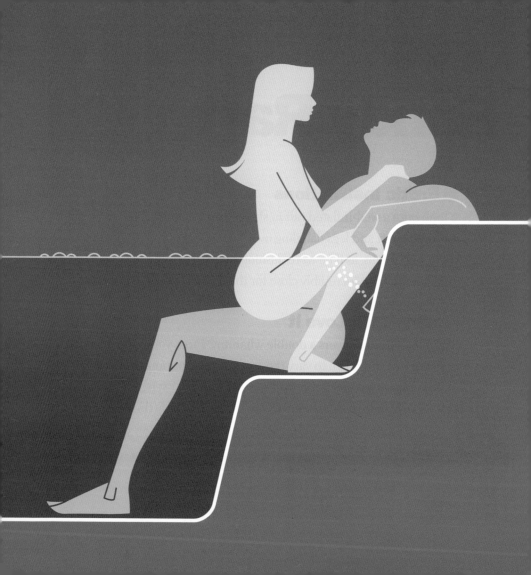

Hot-Tub Hug

■ Erotic Instructions

Start with your guy sitting on the bench with his knees bent and legs slightly spread, leaning back with his arms outstretched and resting on the edge of the tub. Straddle him, facing forward, and lower yourself onto his penis, holding on to his shoulders for support. Keep your knees bent and feet flat as you move up and down or back and forth.

■ Why You'll Love It

The space between your torsos allows both of you to watch the action. There's also room for pelvic play, so you can maximize clitoral stimulation by rubbing your bliss button against his pubic bone as you gyrate.

AQUA EXTRA Take advantage of this you-on-top pose to titillate his pleasure-receptive nipples. Draw gentle circles around them with your fingers as you grind.

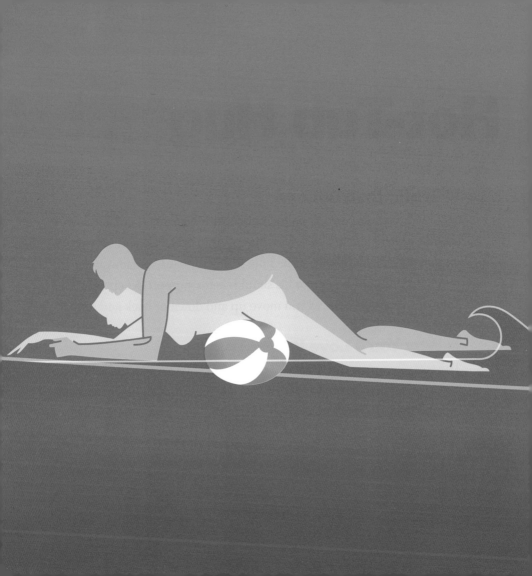

Beach-Ball Booty

■ Erotic Instructions

This position gives a whole new meaning to the phrase "Havin' a ball." With your back to the ocean, lie facedown at the shoreline. Place a beach ball under your pelvis, keeping your legs slightly spread and your arms outstretched in front of you. Your partner lies over you in the same position with his legs together between yours and enters you from behind.

■ Why You'll Love It

With your pelvis elevated by the ball, your man has primo access to your G-spot. The combo of his thrusts and the lapping water against your skin feels downright heavenly.

AQUA EXTRA Dig your toes into the sand to steady yourself. Being anchored gives you better leverage for more passionate pelvic pumping.

A CARNAL
CLASSIC ALL
GUYS CRAVE

Sensual Shower

■ Erotic Instructions

This passionate pose will really steam up your bathroom mirror. Stand facing each other in the shower. Hug your partner as you wrap your left leg around his waist. He places his right hand under your thigh to keep you steady as he enters you. Meanwhile, his other hand is free to caress your face and run his fingers through your hair.

■ Why You'll Love It

You and your guy are up close and personal. Add the water pouring over you and this is a perfect position for lots of wet, passionate kissing. You can also gaze into each other's eyes, further boosting the intimacy factor.

AQUA EXTRA

Have your guy bend his right leg so you can grind your clitoris in small circles against his thigh, sending you into sensory overdrive.

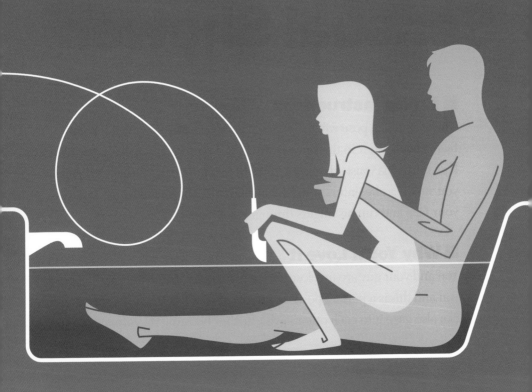

The Rub-a-Dub

■ Erotic Instructions

Your man sits against the back of a tub with his legs as straight and wide as possible. Squat over him, facing his feet, and lower yourself onto his penis, keeping your legs outside of his. Holding on to the edge of the tub for balance, turn on the water and use your free hand to aim a detachable showerhead between your legs. The running water will cascade over your clitoris, adding to the ecstasy.

■ Why You'll Love It

Talk about doubling your pleasure. You get simultaneous internal and clitoral stimulation, and your man's hands are free to fondle the rest of you.

AQUA EXTRA

Don't have a handheld spray? Sit near the faucet and direct the water with your hand. Have your man trail his finger down your spine for a shivery rush.

Booty Blunders

Maximize your Aqua Kama Sutra pleasure by steering clear of these pitfalls. Here's how to avoid them.

Indecent Exposure

Doing the deed outdoors can be exhilarating—just be careful not to get caught in a public place. Our advice: Keep your bathing suit on unless you're sure that you're completely out of sight. You can also wait until dusk or plan your beach romp slightly off-season, when the weather's still warm but crowds have dispersed. And if you're getting busy in the ocean, keep his trunks and your bikini at hand so you can get dressed in a hurry.

Booty Burn

When you fool around while the sun is shining, slather on lots of waterproof SPF 15 or higher or you might end up with burned private parts. Ouch!

Sand Trap

Rolling around with your guy on a deserted beach can be romantic, except for all that sand creeping into your crack. It's not harmful, but it can be very irritating. The best way to spare your nether regions: Keep your movements to a minimum, or better yet, make sure your butt doesn't stray too far from your towel.

Slippery Territory

Tubs and showers can be pretty slippery when they get wet. So remember to always play it safe and use an antislip mat to prevent a wipeout. Plus, it'll provide much-needed cushioning for your knees and elbows as the two of you get busy.

FLUB FIX-ITS

Don't let these water mishaps put a damper
on your pleasure. *Cosmo* comes to the rescue.

THE FLUB	THE FIX
Your bathing-suit bottom washes out to sea.	Cover your private parts by putting together a seaweed bikini.
You get busted by the lifeguard.	Say you were practicing CPR.
You slip and land in a rather embarrassing position.	Inform your man that you're trying out a new naked yoga pose.
You mistakenly queef in the bath.	Tell your dude your tub's a Jacuzzi.
You get bit down there by a crab or some other sea creature.	Have your guy kiss it and make it better.
In a moment of passion, you reach for the shower rod and rip it from the wall.	Laugh it off and say "Oh, I was thinking of redecorating anyway."

DAVID LAWRENCE

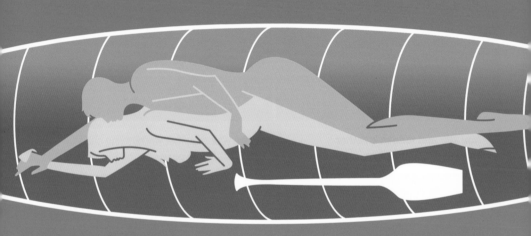

Canoe Canoodle

■ Erotic Instructions

In a canoe or rowboat, paddle a short distance from shore. Once you're at your desired locale, stretch out on your side, resting your head on your bottom arm for cushioning. (Bend your knees if necessary.) Have your partner spoon you from behind, keeping his top arm wrapped around your waist as he enters you and begins to thrust gently.

■ Why You'll Love It

This relaxing pose is perfect for slow, sensuous lovemaking. Because of the close confines, your bodies will be melded from head to toe, and the rocking motion of the boat will intensify each of his internal strokes.

AQUA EXTRA

Take it nice and easy or your boat could tip over. To play it supersafe, make sure you only go out on a calm lake where you can swim to shore.

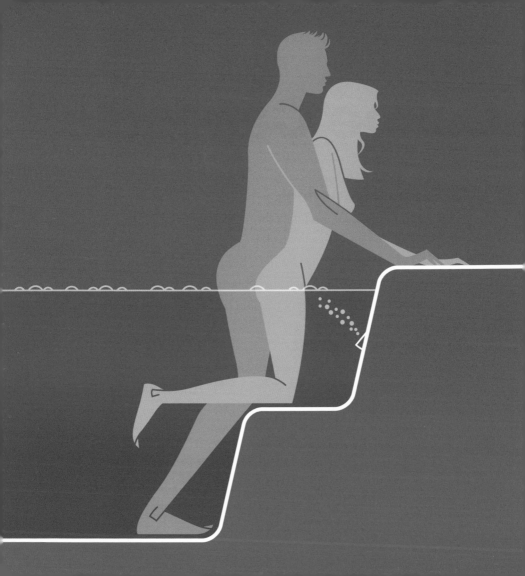

Jet Jiggy

■ Erotic Instructions

Facing a jet, kneel on the seat of a hot tub and lean forward so you're on all fours. Have your partner kneel between your legs so he can enter you from behind. Once he's firmly inside you, both of you should grab on to the edge of the tub to help balance yourselves and slowly straighten up so the two of you are upright. Continue holding on to the tub for support as he pumps away.

■ Why You'll Love It

With your nether regions directly in the jet stream, you get that all-important clitoral friction, helping you sail closer to the O zone.

AQUA EXTRA

If the water pressure begins to cause you discomfort or numbness, use one of your hands to cover the jet and temporarily defer the flow.

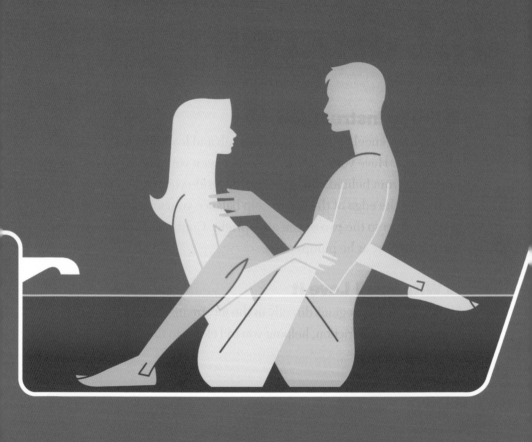

Tub Tangle

■ Erotic Instructions

With your man reclining in a tub full of water, straddle his lap, facing him. Once he's inside you, have him sit up so you're face-to-face. Then, wrap your legs around each other's backs and link your elbows under each other's knees, lifting them to chest level. Hold on to each other tightly as you sway back and forth to ecstasy.

■ Why You'll Love It

Talk about having a romantic romp. This position makes the most of a confined space by allowing you to entwine your bodies and create a cozy connection that's ideal for intense intimacy.

AQUA EXTRA

Since your mouths are in such close proximity, indulge in lots of passionate smooching. Don't forget to nibble on tasty tidbits like his ears and neck.

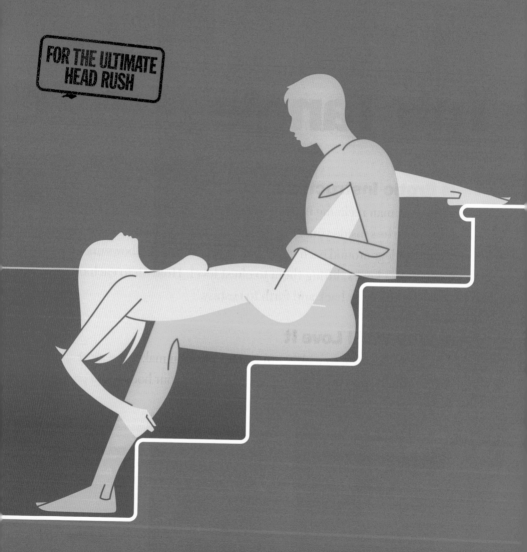

FOR THE ULTIMATE
HEAD RUSH

Submarine

■ Erotic Instructions

Have your man sit on the second or third stair in the shallow end of the pool (or on the hot-tub bench). Straddle his lap and take him inside you. Next, lift your legs so your feet are propped up on the top of the stairs. Have him grab on to your thighs as you lean back. Hold on to his calves to help you stay elevated as he pulls you back and forth.

■ Why You'll Love It

The feeling of weightlessness combined with the sensual depravation of not being able to hear since your ears are submerged will allow you to surrender to the bliss of your partner's member throbbing inside you.

AQUA EXTRA

Hone your erotic sensory perception even further by closing your eyes. The more senses you stifle, the more intensely you'll experience the others.

The Sea Horse

■ Erotic Instructions

Have your man lie on his back, facing the ocean, with his legs straight out in front of him and in the water. He can prop himself up on his forearms if he doesn't want to get his hair full of sand. Straddle his lap while facing away from him and slowly lower yourself onto his member. Rest your hands on his pelvic area or thighs to help propel you.

■ Why You'll Love It

This passion position allows for deliciously deep penetration—and gives your guy a mouthwatering view of your bootie bobbing up and down—as the ocean washes over your bottom halves.

AQUA EXTRA Since you're in charge of the randy reins, lean your torso forward or backward to alter the depth and angle of penetration as you ride him.

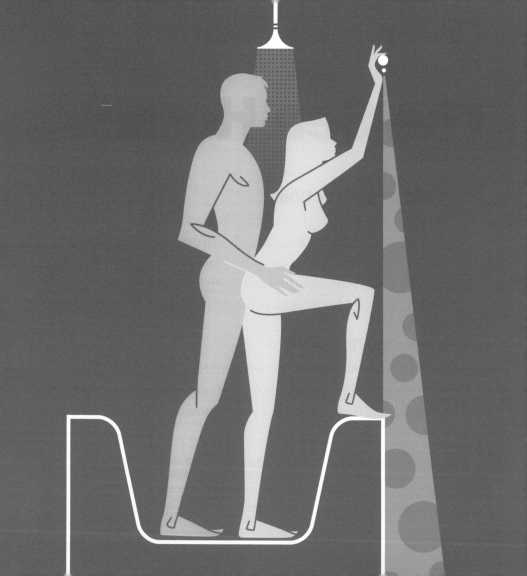

The Hot Rod

■ Erotic Instructions

Place an antislip bath mat in a tub with a showerhead. Then stand facing the curtain with the liner outside the tub. Rest one foot on the edge of the tub as you reach up and check that the rod is securely fastened to the wall. If so, grip the rod with both hands to steady yourself (not to hang on). Your man holds your waist as he enters you from behind.

■ Why You'll Love It

This hands-on-the-rod pose gives your guy free rein to explore every inch of your body as the water cascades over both of you. And since you can't anticipate his next move, every caress will be a sultry surprise.

AQUA EXTRA

When you feel an O building, have your man grab onto your butt and squeeze hard for extra skin-tingling pressure.

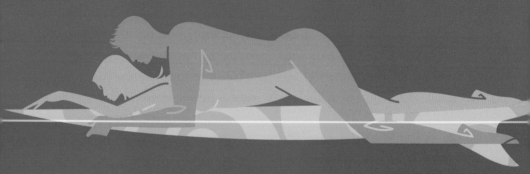

Surf's Up

■ Erotic Instructions

This is a tricky pose and can only be done when the sea is calm. Lie facedown on a surfboard with your arms and legs outstretched on either side. With your guy standing at your side in waist-deep water, have him wrap his leg around the board to mount it like a horse and enter you from behind. Once he and the board are steady, he should stretch out as well.

■ Why You'll Love It

Trying not to tip over the surfboard adds an extra element of fun to this carnal challenge. And, having the hard substance beneath you—and his hard body on top of you—feels exquisitely sexy.

AQUA EXTRA

To avoid a wipeout, minimize your movements. Flex your Kegels (muscles you use to hold back urine) to create waves of pleasure.

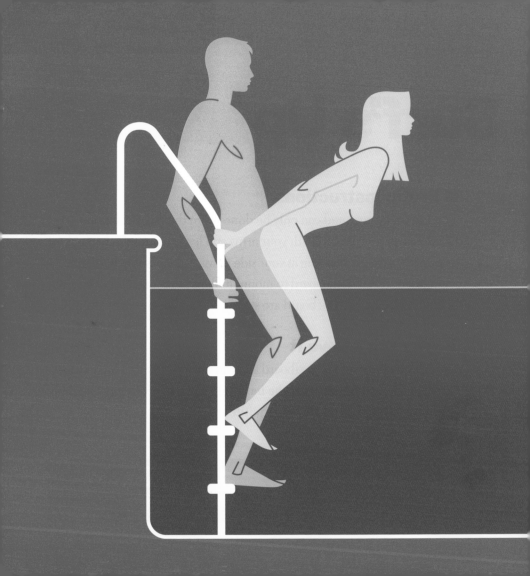

Ladder Lovin'

■ Erotic Instructions

This position requires some maneuvering. Climb down to the second-to-last rung of the pool ladder. Do a 180, holding the rails, so your back is to the wall. Lean forward and spread your legs so your guy can lower himself behind you and place his feet between your legs on the rung below you. Adjust your bodies so he can slip himself inside you.

■ Why You'll Love It

In this half-in, half-out-of-the-water position, only your lower bodies are submerged. So each time your man thrusts, cold water will splash against your exposed skin, electrifying all of your nerve endings.

AQUA EXTRA

To avoid doing a belly flop into the water, hold tight and gently gyrate your pelvis in small circles instead of wildly bucking up and down.

Copyright © 2006 by Hearst Communications, Inc.

Edited by JOHN SEARLES
Book Design by PETER PERRON
Text by JANE KATZ and MEAGHAN BUCHAN

Editor in Chief: KATE WHITE
Design Director: ANN P. KWONG

Library of Congress Cataloging-in-Publication Data Available.

10 9 8 7 6 5 4 3 2

Published by Hearst Books
A Division of Sterling Publishing Co., Inc.
387 Park Avenue South, New York, NY 10016

Cosmopolitan and Hearst Books are registered trademarks of Hearst Communications, Inc.

cosmopolitan.com

DuraBook™, patent no. 6,773,034, is a trademark of Melcher Media, Inc., 124 West 13th Street, New York, NY 10011, melcher.com. The DuraBook™ format utilizes revolutionary technology and is completely waterproof and highly durable.

For information about custom editions, special sales, and premium and corporate purchases, please contact Sterling Special Sales Department at 800-805-5489 or specialsales@sterlingpub.com.

Distributed in Canada by Sterling Publishing
c/o Canadian Manda Group, 165 Dufferin Street
Toronto, Ontario, Canada M6K 3H6

Distributed in Australia by Capricorn Link (Australia) Pty. Ltd.
PO Box 704, Windsor, NSW 2756 Australia

Manufactured in Hong Kong

Sterling ISBN 13: 978-158816-571-8
ISBN 10: 1-58816-571-X